W9-CBV-301

11-99

Bugs and Critters I Have Known

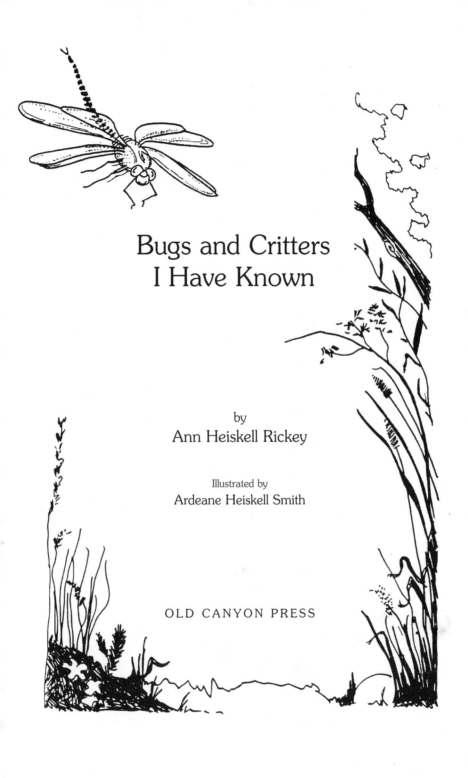

Bugs and Critters
I Have Known

by
Ann Heiskell Rickey

Illustrated by
Ardeane Heiskell Smith

OLD CANYON PRESS

Published by

OLD CANYON PRESS
2865 Marquette Drive
Topanga, California 90290

Copyright © 1999 by Ann Heiskell Rickey

Bugs and Critters I Have Known
by
Ann Heiskell Rickey

Illustrated by
Ardeane Heiskell Smith

Summary: An illustrated collection of fifty humorous
verses about bugs and sea creatures.

1. Children's Poetry, American

Edited by *Lamar Hawkins*
Designed by *Cheryl Carrington*

ISBN: 0-9667834-1-7
Library of Congress Catalog Card Number: 98-68083

First edition

Printed in the United States of America

For Caitlin, Jarren and Jaci

Table of Contents

PART ONE

Bugs I Have Known
11

PART TWO
Critters of the Sea and Shore
73

Introduction

Here's a book about bugs, bad bugs and good bugs,
Plain bugs, strange bugs, misunderstood bugs,
Fat bugs, lean bugs, nice bugs, mean bugs,
Fuzzy bugs, slick bugs, even unseen bugs.
Some stories are true, or at least they could be.
Some stories aren't true, but perhaps they should be.
Entomologically, most are quite proper
But once in a while I will tell a real whopper.
Do I have you confused? Good! You're on your own.
Now I'd like you to meet some bugs I have known. ◆

PART ONE
Bugs I Have Known

Chiggers

How do the chiggers supply their needs
Unless I go walking through the weeds? ◆

Lady Bug

Lady Bug, Lady Bug, don't fly away,
My roses have aphids, I beg you to stay;
Your house is not burning, your children are fine,
Lady Bug, Lady Bug, sit down and dine.◆

Bumblebees

I'm well aware that bumblebees
Get pollen on their hairy knees
But would you kindly tell me, please,
Why I've never seen one sneeze? ◆

The Centipede

Let's talk about legs. Well, birds have two,
Lizards and animals four.
Insects do their tricks with six
But a centipede has legs galore.

How does he keep them all in a row,
All on one side straight or angled?
And if he should trip on a pebble or twig,
How would he get them untangled?

But no, he won't stumble, he's choreographed,
Always in step and in time,
And as he completes these feats with his feet
He's a one-arthropod chorus line.

He can hustle or shuffle or tango or jive,
And one other knack's kind of nifty:
If anyone says to him, "Gimme five,"
He can easily give 'em fifty. ◆

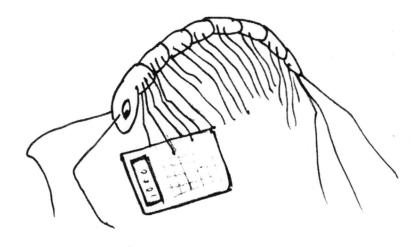

16

The Mayfly

A mayfly, you guessed it, is born in May.
But did you know she lives only one day?
When she opens her eyes to the morning sun,
Her first and her last day have begun.

One morning a mayfly was drying her wings
On a stalk that held two other new things.
One was a stinkbug of mean disposition,
The other an ant, a young politician.

The ant said, "Now that your wings are unfurled,
Welcome, sweet Mayfly, to the world.
And let me, please, be the first to say,
In all sincerity, have a nice day."

The stinkbug was filled with a bitter self-pity
And madly jealous of anything pretty.
She made a remark that would cut like a knife,
"It's the very last day of the rest of your life."

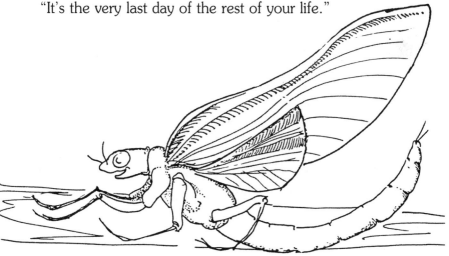

The mayfly shrugged, it was best to forgive it.
Whatever her time, she was now off to live it.
She only returned when the sun was sinking;
The ant was washing, the stinkbug stinking.

The ant said, "Hello, and hip, hip, hip hooray!
Well, let me tell you about my day.
There were so many tasks that I just stopped countin'.
I dug a subway and moved a mountain.

"Stayed busier far than the busiest bee,
And all for the good of the colony.
I've touched antennas with 'most every member
And asked them to vote for me come November.

"I took not one minute to stop and play.
But let's ask the stinkbug, 'How was your day?'"
The stinkbug was sunk in a deep purple funk,
"Well, most of the time I just sat here and stunk."

"Well, it takes all kinds," said the ant. "And so,
Tell us, sweet Mayfly, how did it go?"

"I'm sure, Mr. Ant, you will think me a shirk
'Cause I didn't do one solid lick of work.
For all of us born on this date in May
Decided we'd dance the day away.

"And over a meadow full of flowers
We twirled and spiraled for hours and hours.
Up we'd swirl, and around and around,
And when we got tired, we'd kind of float down.

"Ms. Stinkbug will judge that my time was wasted,
But most of the sweets of life I've tasted.
I watched a rabbit lining her nest,
Saw a fox on the run and a fawn at rest.

"Got tossed around by a friendly breeze
And smelled the blooms of the apricot trees.
Then I paused to leave my eggs behind,
Ensuring the future of mayfly kind.

"I've basked in the sun and bathed in the rain,
But I've broken no promises, caused no pain,
Made no enemies, left no debts,
So, all in all, I have no regrets."

The ant replied, "You're uncivilized,
But I doubt your day should be criticized
For those whose lives are transitory
Are touched with a special kind of glory.

"Now the sun has set, the moon's on the rise,
The time has come for our last goodbyes."
The stinkbug, then, to her utter surprise,
Suddenly found she had tears in her eyes. ◆

Silver Fishes

Now let us consider the silver fishes:
They run very fast with some side-to-side swishes,
The bindings of books are their favorite dishes,
But anything starched they find just as delicious.

They haven't got wings like those little wool moths
But, similarly, they're addicted to cloths.
If you open a drawer and one scoots to a corner,
Your very best shirt is most likely a goner.

Now, an archivist or a loyal librarian
Would rather not serve as their dietarian.
If, checking a treasure, one plops in her lap
He might be digesting a priceless old map.

They're lacking in taste, they'd as soon ingest
A folio Shakespeare as Edgar Guest.
So, a lover of books, if given three wishes,
Might spend one disposing of silver fishes. ◆

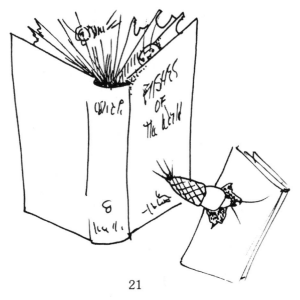

21

Doodle Bugs

A curly, jet black, standard poodle
Looking for some doggy boodle
Turned a rock up with his noodle
And guess what he found?

Just oodles
Of doodles. ◆

The Caterpillar

A caterpillar named Priscilla
Asked her friend, the armadillo,
If she'd share a sasparilla
Stirred with honey and vanilla.

They sat beneath a weeping willow,
A puffball for Priscilla's pillow.
Her guest, whose given name was Lida,
Found a moss bed close beside her.

They laughed and gossiped and sipped their tea
And Lida recited some poetry.
They made up their own little rhymes and jokes
Lampooning various garden folks.

Priscilla invented a limerick
About a squirrel and a walking stick,
And Lida composed a villanelle
About a coon and a cockerel.

Their afternoon was fancyfree
'Til Priscilla glanced to the top of the tree
And felt a dreadful horror fill her
There was Joe, the crow, the vicious killer.

To a crow Priscilla would be a prize.
Joe carefully focused his beady eyes;
His wings unfolded, his yellow bill
Was aimed straight down to make the kill.

Priscilla cried, "I think he spied me!"
Said Lida calmly, "Come inside me."
Knowing Joe could never harm her
Under armadillo armor.

But now Priscilla had to race
To reach dear Lida's carapace.
She stumbled on a willow shoot
And tripped upon a root to boot.

Her forward progress was painfully slow.
The same could never be said for Joe.
He reached Mach Four as he dove pellmell.
Priscilla just touched the edge of the shell.

But now she was giving her personal best;
Her head went in and some of her chest;
She pushed and pulled 'til wonder of wonder
Twelve of her segments scuttled under.

And then Priscilla lost her luck,
The tip of her tail had somehow got stuck
But Lida goaded, "Come on! You're a worm-
If nothing else you are able to squirm."

Priscilla twisted and shimmied and wriggled
'Til, plip, she was in! Then she curled up and giggled,
Warm and safe and sound at last.
But Joe kept coming, terribly fast

And now his speed achieved Mach Five
In his hungry, predatory dive.
He did not waver, he did not swerve,
You couldn't fault him for lack of nerve,

But from brain too weak or from too much pride
He split his beak on Lida's hide.
They heard him croaking, "Curses! Curses!
I despise you both and I hate your verses." ◆

Mealy Bugs

The top's snug and tight on my cereal bin,
So how did the mealy bugs ever get in? ◆

The Earwig

An earwig has nothing to do with wigs,
But you'll never persuade Miss Elvira T. Higgs.
She's aware that it isn't a hairpiece or rug,
Toupée or peruke; it is only a bug.

But once she saw pictures: its claws are behind—
Contrary to nature! The sight blew her mind.
For what other creatures have claws on their rears?
It was not only strange but a danger to ears.

She's not the first human to harbor such fears:
The bug's reputation spans hundreds of years.
Miss Higgs but enlarged on the ancient horrifics
And added her own rather gaudy specifics.

Suppose she should purchase a moviestar wig—
One would crawl in her cavity, back up and dig,
From whence it would burrow straight into her brain
And certainly cause both confusion and pain.

That's not at all true but you'll never convince her;
When pondering pincers, Miss Higgs is a wincer.
And though she has now gone as bald as a bone,
Not a sprig of a wig will Miss Higgs ever own. ◆

The Spittle Bug

The spittle bug
Is a little bug
Whose skin is terribly sunburn prone.
But tender or not
He's not in a spot
To go to the drugstore for Coppertone.

But he never gets burned
For somehow he's learned
How best to avoid any blister troubles:
On a stem he'll sit,
Then he'll spit and he'll spit
'Til he totally covers himself with
    bubbles.

Any redhead out there
Who is freckled or fair,
Make like a spittle bug, save your
    hide!
Umbrellas and cloth
Aren't as handy as froth
But you too, if bare, can be
    sizzled and fried. ◆

The Caddis Worm

The caddis worm lives where the great trout swim.
They're a danger to him
And his chances are slim.

So he cannily covers his back with twigs
And rubbish and sprigs
And thingamajigs.

Then glad as a pig his life is spent
Under his tent.
It's no accident.

For what is the purpose of all that debris?
Well, it naturally
Makes him hard to see.

And a Rainbow out scouting to find his lunch
Might well have a hunch
And think, "Munch, munch!

"I'd love me a nice juicy worm to smash
And mash into hash—
But I won't eat trash!" ◆

The Luna Moth

A Luna Moth is a pale, soft green,
The loveliest color you've ever seen.
Once when I was about thirteen
I captured one. I took some screen
And quarter rounds and made a box,
Then gave her water, leaves and rocks.

She settled down, accepting fate,
As if to rest—or as if to wait.
I put her on the window sill
And went to sleep that night until
A thump, thump, thumping reached my ear,
Like a muffled drum or a heart in fear.

The only light was a spindly moon
But something was trying to get in the room.
It took but a moment to recognize
The swallow tails, the big false eyes.
The Luna male had come for his lass
And was beating himself to death on the glass.

His wings were tattered, his velvety nap
Was dusting the pane with each frenzied flap:
A gentle thing turned strong and wild
Like a mother who fights to protect a child.
Did he know or care that he charged in vain,
That his tender body could not break the pane?

I couldn't bear his fierce rampage,
I pushed up the window and opened her cage.
She fluttered a moment, tentatively,
As if not sure she was truly free.
And then she was soaring in perfect flight
To join her lover, her prince, her knight.

I watched them, together, flying high,
Silhouetted against the sky.
That was long, long ago but I've never again
Imprisoned a wild thing in a pen. ◆

Some Warnings

If you should encounter a yellow jacket,
Pack it!

If you see a bee protecting his wax,
Make tracks!

If a dirt dauber seems to be aiming at you,
Toddleoo!

If a hornet is buzzing around your ear,
Advance to the rear.

The rule is: Near anything armed with a stinger
       Don't linger. ◆

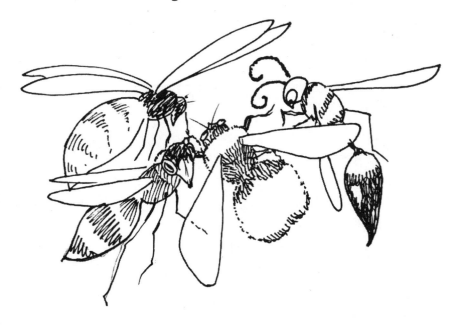

The Tomato Worms

Fred's a tomato worm, Ned's his twin;
Fred's pretty fat and Ned's not thin.
They live in the garden of Mr. X. Urb
And their appetites aren't easy to curb.

They're perfectly matched to tomato plant green
So that under the leaves they can hardly be seen.
But they're tempted by fruit that has ripened to red
And this is a danger for Fred and Ned.

Green on red isn't camouflage,
A situation they normally dodge
By getting up early when days are dewy,
When men are asleep and tomatoes are chewy.

Now Fred is a clever ventriloquist
So, venturing out in the morning mist,
Between big bites of a firm tomato
Fred practiced his art with quotations from Plato.

"'Injustice is always an evil,'" he said,
And it seemed to come from the turnip green bed.
"'There's absolute beauty and absolute good',"
And it came from behind a cordon of wood.

Ned praised him, "You're great at ventriloquy."
Fred said, "I'll try Hamlet's *Soliloquy*.
'To be or not to be, that is the question.'
But—burp—I'm so full I've got indigestion.

"That line was aimed straight at a lettuce head
But it came from a sunflower bloom instead."
Mr. Urb was awakened by all this squawking.
He thought, "Are my veggies suddenly talking?

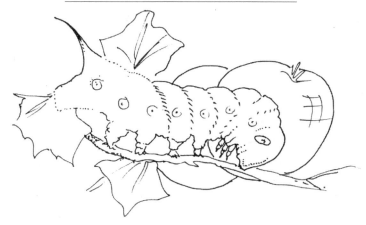

"Or could there be thieves in my fine tomatoes
Out stealing to stock their refrigerators?
I'd better go check on them, just to be sure."
Then Fred gave up spouting good literature

And noted, "Smack, smack! These tomatoes are luscious.
But, yipes! Mr. Urb's on his way. He'll sqush us.
We stand out like zits on these red tomatoes.
Oh, I wish we were prestidigitators."

But worms can't make themselves disappear.
Whenever they move, they move in low gear.
Mr. Urb crept up close to them, glowering down
With a menacing, sinister, threatening frown.

"Something's been eating my prize tomatoes!"
Fred threw his voice and yelled, "Alligators!"
"Alligators?" the gardener exclaimed,
"That's the very last thing I would ever have blamed.

"I'll go get my gun to repulse their attack."
And deciding on this, Mr. Urb turned his back
And before he had figured what wasn't quite right
The worms had wormed themselves out of sight. ◆

Monarchs

Winds go chill in late September
Hinting frost, foretelling snow.
Monarchs one and all remember
Summer's going. They must go.

One last drink of honey nectar,
One last taste of pollen. Then,
Pointing on a Southwest vector,
Monarchs take to wing again.

Hard the journey they've begun,
Long the way: two thousand miles.
There's a race that must be won
Whether nature frowns or smiles.

Thousands join them one by one.
Men look up and shade their eyes.
Something's blotting out the sun—
A cloud? A cloud of butterflies.

Now they're flying treetop low,
Now they flutter, now they glide.
If a norther starts to blow
Up they rise and take a ride.

Carried fast before the storm,
Aided by the frigid flow,
Always heading toward the warm,
Heading South to Mexico.

Over mountains, over plains,
Over water, desert land,
There's a compass in their brains
No mere man can understand.

With, against, across the wind,
Buffeted, they never stray;
Like an army disciplined
Not to turn and run away.

Oh, they are determined things,
Dawn to dusk and dusk to dawn,
Testing tiring, fragile wings
Traveling, traveling, traveling on.

Flying true and flying fast
Though it takes a hundred days
'Til they've reached the spot at last
Where they'll rest and drink and laze.

(You can visit they're on view,
Millions in their winter home.
Take a jet. An hour or two
Covers all the miles they've flown.)

April now. No snows are falling
On the fields they used to know.
Softer days are calling, calling.
Summer's coming. They must go.

One last sip of honey nectar
One last taste of pollen. Then,
Pointing on a Northeast vector
Monarchs take to wing again.

Hard the journey they've begun
Long the way . . . long the way . . . ◆

Viceroy Butterfly

To a Jay a Monarch tastes nasty, tastes awful.
He'll go a long way to avoid a craw full.
So if Monarchs live easy
By making birds queasy
Then imitation is perfectly lawful.

Now take a good look at a Viceroy:
His taste is precisely what Jays would enjoy
But he's orange and black
And he looks exact-
Ly like a Monarch, a masterful ploy.

A Jaybird out hunting is torn with doubt:
Which is the one he would have to spit out?
Which one is sweet
As the finest mincemeat
And which one is yucky as sauerkraut? ◆

The Flu Bug

You're lying in bed in a damp nightgown
And you feel like a mangy, fleabitten hound;
Then the doctor says with a little frown,
"It's just that bug that is going around."

A bug that's causing these pains and aches?
These sniffles and coughs, these sweats and shakes—
A bug that you can't even see or touch—
An invisible bug? Well, that's too much!

The doctor says, "No need for anxiety.
I'm sure it's a flu of the Asian variety.
Stay flat on your back. In a day or two
You'll find that you're practically good as new."

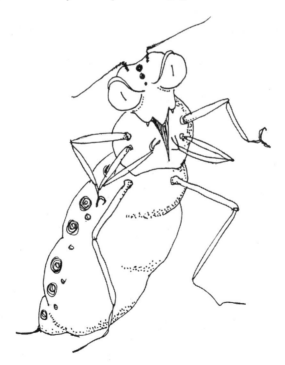

You don't believe him. You think you're dying.
You ask yourself, "Was the flu bug flying
Or swimming or skimming across the sea
Those thousands of miles to end up in me?"

So with nothing better to do than be quiet
You let your imagination run riot
And picture the bug that's your misery's cause:
Does he have six eyes and scissory jaws?

Or is he a monster from outer space
With arms and legs but no head and no face?
Or a scaly dragon whose tongue spits lasers,
Or a grinning baboon whose fingers are razors?

Or is he perhaps just a green glob of goo
That oozes around in the creases of you?
Or a purple snake so slithery, creepy . . .
But now you are getting

                    t
                  e
               r
                r
                  i   s
                    b   l
                    l   e
                  y   e
                            p
                        y . . . ◆

The Ant Lion

The ant lion lives in a conical pit
At the bottom of which he will quietly sit
'Til an ant falls down, then lickety-split
He'll chomp and make a meal of it.
Now here's the way you can outwit
An ant lion. Make a small tidbit
Of mud that's formed of dust and spit,
Then find a straw that will perfectly fit
And cover the tip of the straw with the grit.
Now poke it slowly down the slit.
When you feel a tug, your ant lion has hit!
So pull him right up. He's an ugly crit-
Ter that well might frighten a baby sit-
Ter. Or anyone else you will have to admit.
Well, I've totally run out of rhymes.

I quit! ◆

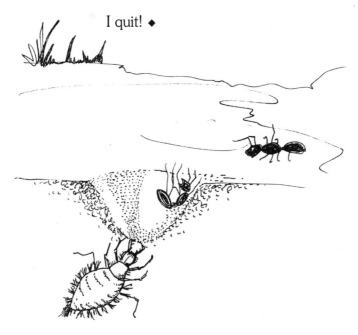

Flies, Mosquitoes, and Fleas

I've often thought, if I had two vetoes
The choice would be easy: flies and
    mosquitoes.
These two I am sure we could well
    do without.
Then . . . I think about flycatchers,
    think about trout,
Think about bullfrogs, martins and swallows.
Would they go hungry? And, if so, what follows?
Mosquitoes and flies are their principal diet—
No songs in the morning? I'd pine from the quiet.

So that's reason enough to put
    up with these.
Now I'm thinking again. Okay,
    take away fleas.
They're good for nothing except
    to irk us.
Well . . . yes, I've seen trained
    ones in the circus;
They've not much talent and even less style
But watch the little children smile!
Then what is of value and
    what is a pest?
And just who am I to think I
    know best? ◆

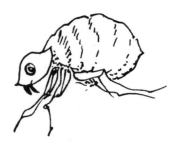

Water Striders

I find that I am especially fond
Of the water striders on my pond.
They glide on the surface with ballet-star ease
As if slaloming on six little skis. ◆

The Dragon Fly

A dragon fly hovers
On cellophane wings,
Like fairies and elves
And nice, friendly things.
His back's jewel-bright,
He's as tame as can be;
If you sit by a pond,
He might light on your knee.
So his name then is nothing
But folderol,
For he doesn't resemble
A dragon at all.
In the South people call him
A Snake Doctor. Wow!
Could he doctor a snake?
Well I fail to see how.
Then can we agree
Both those names are a shame
And think of our own
More appropriate name?
Watch as he sits on a lily pad.
There!
He's not just a bug,
He's enamel, he's air,
He's gossamer lace,
He's a shimmering dandy,

He's emeralds, turquoise
And spun sugar candy.
But the names that I've thought of
Are wronger than wrong,
They're either too fancy,
Too short or too long,
So get set to help me—
It's one, two, three, go!
If you hit on the right one,
Please let me know. ◆

The Slug

A slug
Is a slimy bug
There is nothing quite so ug-
Ly as a slug.

A slug
Is a lonely bug
Cause what would ever want to hug
A slug? ◆

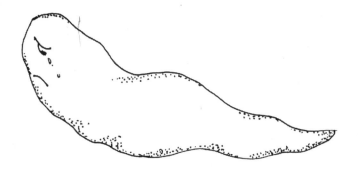

The Beetle

To be turned on his back
To a beetle is hateful;

Turn him back over—
He'll be truly grateful. ◆

The Boll Weevil

To a southern farmer there's nothing as evil
As Anthronomus Grandis, the cotton boll weevil.
As larva, as pupa, as grownup he's rotten:
He lives in the pods and chews up the cotton.

But look! There's a biplane flying low,
Spraying the summer fields row on row.
Those sneaky old weevils will soon be forgotten
And the bolls will unfold into fluffy white cotton.

But what of the poisons the plane left behind?
Do they stay in the ground? And should we mind?
And what are those stinky fumes in the air?
What else do they kill? And should we care? ◆

The Tarantula

To Ed a dog was ordinary,
He wanted something truly scary,
Something wild and weird and different,
Something horribly magnificent.

He had no room for a Bengal tiger,
Panther, leopard, lion or liger:
Instead he bought a large tarantula
And named his hairy pet Gargantua.

At first Ed fed him ants and flies
But the spider rapidly grew in size
'Til after a while he came to prefer
Barbecued pork and hamburger.

Gargantua wasn't so hard to keep:
Most of the while he was fast asleep.
He lived in a closet under the stair
Unless he lounged on the overstuffed chair.

So any friend who came to visit
Might plan to sit, then shriek, "What is it?"
Or, hanging a raincoat in the closet,
Might faint and reviving, squeak, "What was it?"

Ed tickled the feet of his hirsute fella
'Til he danced a passable tarantella.
Ed taught him then to perform this antic
Until it drove his relatives frantic.

Gargantua finally got so fat
That he looked like a fuzzy, six-legged cat.
Then Ed took him walking on a leash
And together they'd dance a Scottish schottische.

All four-legged animals crept to hide,
All two-legged animals kept inside,
Except for a jogger so taken aback
That he had a serious panic attack.

Ed laughed at them all. He got his kicks
By playing such devilish little tricks.
What most people thought was mean and contrarious
To Ed was just howlingly hilarious.

What Ed wouldn't admit was that spider anxiety
Inflicts a majority in society.
To anyone who's a whit fastidious
The tiniest spider is downright hideous;

And larger specimens grossly insidious—
Their habits, too, are considered invidious.
Ed also forgot that: To be perfidious
Is the nature of all things arachnideous.

And now, dear reader, here comes the clincher:
That bug got as big as a Doberman Pinscher.
Then came the day Ed reached out to pet him
And guess what happened? Gargantua et him. ◆

The Praying Mantis

The praying mantis stifled a yawn
And picked her teeth on a minuscule thorn.
When I meekly inquired what it was that she ate,
She replied, "That was Hal, my delicious late mate."

I was slightly embarrassed, but why should I mind?
It was normal behavior for mantis kind.
I needed to change the subject matter,
To praise her endeavors, to thank her, to flatter—

For all day long she deftly devours
The baneful bugs that munch on my flowers.
Unfortunately I didn't put it quite right
I said, "I salute your appetite.

You're very efficient at husbandry."
She scowled. "Are you making fun of me?"
"No, I didn't mean that," I said, "Beg pardon.
I meant that you're such a help in the garden."

"You're forgiven," she said. "We've made our deals.
Your plants are providing my everyday meals.
Just promise as long as I deign to reside here
You'll never, ever, spray pesticide here.

"I'm cheaper than DDT for gardeners,
So you and I are kind of partners."
I couldn't explain, but she's more than that.
What doesn't pollute the habitat,

No longer old-fashioned and out of date,
Is a way of living I celebrate.
I've the deepest respect for
    the praying mantis. She
Is my friend, my helper
    . . . my fantasy.

Honey Bees

A bee stung Caity. She sniffled and said,
"I wish every bee in the world were dead."
But later that day when her father came home
He raided the hive and took out the comb.
And then they had pancakes smothered with honey
That she wouldn't have traded for love or for money.
She licked sticky fingers and said, "I forgive,
And I wish every bee in the world would live." ◆

The Snail

"With my house on my back
I don't need to pack
To go on a trip," said the snail;
"But if you wish to find me
There's a clue right behind
me—
Just follow my silvery trail." ◆

The Cricket

It's very bad luck to smush a cricket.
What you must do is carefully pick it
Up in your hand and gently flick it
Out on the lawn where it belongs.

There's no guarantee that it won't return.
Sometimes it seems that crickets yearn
To be inside where they can earn
Fans for their clickety-crickety songs.

When you are trying to get to sleep
And one's strumming away while you're counting sheep,
You'll think of a toilet bowl, dank and deep
And the flush that could end your aggravation.

But they're treasured as pets by many Chinese
And kept in brass boxes with filigrees.
What sings with its wings and
    hears with its knees
Is worth considerable
    admiration. ◆

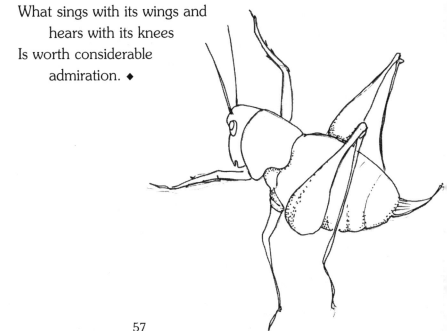

Assassin Bug

There's a bug that is called the Assassin.
I will mention him only in passin'—
    He's both vampiristic
    And cannibalistic
Which is truly a rather low-class sin. ◆

NoSeeEms

You won't find noseeems
In insect museums;
They're either too small
Or . . . they're not there at all. ◆

The Cockroach

For millions of years the cockroach has ranged
All over the earth. He remains little changed.

Now History tells us the Story of Man,
But cockroaches flourished before man began.

So if you've a mind to impress your teacher
Call a cockroach a "prehistoric" creature.

And scientists say that a nuclear war
Would end with the cockroach as strong as before.

For man, I'm afraid, couldn't possibly rival
The cockroach's marvelous art of survival.

So let us be careful whatever we do
Or the cockroach will be "post-historic" too. ◆

The Cicada

There's a kind of cicada
That looks like Darth Vader
With a cold, metal face: no nose and no ears.
They come by the millions,
The billions, the zillions.
Once every seventeen years,
My dears,
Only once every seventeen years.

At the moment of birth
They come out of the earth,
Then they climb up a tree and shuck off their shells.
These are easy to find
Little ghosts left behind
That remind you of hoodoos and spells,
Ma'mselles,
Remind you of witches and spells.

But it's what they do next
That can get people hexed:
They start up a rhythmical, tuneless set;
A shrill kind of humming,
And ear-grating strumming
That's loud as a jumbo jet,
My pet,
Quite as loud as a jumbo jet.

In the late afternoon
They will stridently croon,
And the warmer the weather, the more noise they make.
So I've got an inkling

All that Rip Van Winkling
Made them eager to shout, "I'm awake,"
No mistake,
"Hey, listen up world, I'm awake."

With the frost they'll be gone
But the cycle goes on
And the eggs that they've left on the trees will fall down.
These larval cicadas,
The future invaders,
Dig themselves deep in the ground,
Little clowns,
Dig deep in the cold, hard ground.

And there they will stay
'Til that long away day,
They won't chirrup or squeak or whisper or snore.
No, they won't make a peep;
They'll do nothing but sleep
'Til the summer of twenty one four,
What a bore,
'Til the summer of 2014.◆

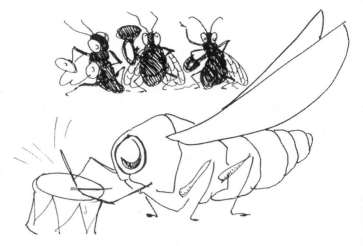

Lice

Lice
Aren't nice.
If they get in your hair
Don't despair
There is hope:
It's called chamomile soap.◆

The Tick

A tick
Can prick
And then he'll stick.
So pick him off quick
Or he might make you sick. ◆

The Woolly Bear

If it's reddish brown with a wide
black band
And has lots of hair
It's a woolly bear.

If you barely touch it with your hand,
It will curl up tight
In a ball from fright.

It's got no tail and it's got no head;
You'd be willing to swear
The poor woolly bear
Is plumb undone and incurably dead.

But once you've gone, he uncurls his frizziness
And goes right on about his business.♦

The Inchworm and the Walking Stick

An inchworm was inching his way along
The twisted stems of a scuppernong,
Heading, apparently, anywhere
But measuring distance
    from here to there.

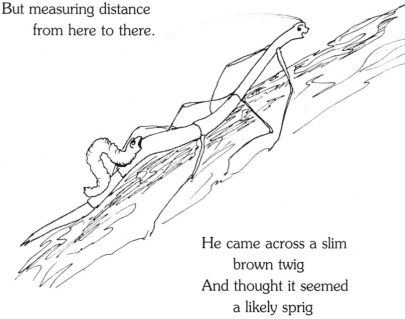

He came across a slim
    brown twig
And thought it seemed
    a likely sprig
The view from which might reward the trip.
Just two or three lengths and he'd be at the tip.

He was humping along on his chosen track
When a voice called out, "Get off my back!"
A closer look made him realize
That the sprig had wings and legs and eyes.

He said, "I'm sorry. That's quite a trick
I could have sworn you were only a stick."
"Well, I'm not," said the walking stick. "Please dismount.
I'm giving you ten and I'm starting to count.

"I mimic sticks for my own protection.
And I'll pass any stupid bird's inspection.
But it's hard to keep this perfect pose
When your little feet are tickling my nose.

"So find yourself another switch.
You're giving me one horrendous itch."
The inchworm said, "I'll go. I'll go.
But please have patience. I'm kind of slow.

"Each step requires that I bunch and hunch,
Then gingerly, pokily unscrunch.
Oh, I wish my gait weren't so shillyshally
But that's my fate, I dillydally."

The stick exploded a huge "Achoo!"
And thrown from his back the inchworm flew
As though from a catapult, high in the sky.
He squealed, "Good gracious! I've learned to fly.

"Here's a lazy eight, some banks, some slips,
A loop-the-loop and some double flips.
A nice chandelle. Oh, no, it's a stall!"
And he headed down in a nosedive fall.

But before he could feel really chickenhearted
He landed exactly where he had started.
The walking stick growled, "I'm counting to ten."
"That's great," said the inchworm. "Do it again!" ◆

The Brown Recluse Spider

Beware of a Brown Recluse Spider
She is deadly and mean and a hider:
    She'll lie waiting to chew
    In your boot or your shoe
'Cause she can't stand a toe alongside her.

No tootsy is safe with this cutie;
To check on your footwear's a duty.
    In the Southwest it's best
    To make a small test:
Before pulling it on, shake your bootie. ◆

The Stag Beetle

With branching antlers on his forehead
He looks more marvelous than horrid.
They're really jaws. (The name is mandible.)
But still his name is understandable.
As any proud, majestic buck
Will tend to leave us wonder struck
Although a head so heavycrowned
Must be a drag to tote around.
And, furthermore, this beetle rarity,
To stags has one more similarity:
To win a bride two males will fight.
Now you must know that's quite a sight. ◆

Fireflies

Fireflies on a summer night
Make us shiver with delight,
Twinkling in the evening's darkling,
Tiny taillights winking, sparkling.

Do they look alike to you?
Look again, it isn't true.
This one blinks a little stronger;
That one holds his lightning longer.

So they are of different species,
Each clan to its own caprices.
Strangely, though, they all are males,
Advertising with their tails.

Perched below, a glow worm glows,
Keenly watching the Romeos.
She is Juliet, she must answer
When she spots her special dancer.

Though she has no wings to fly
She must find the right reply.
What's the signal this one sends?
Which are strangers, which are friends?

It's a riddle unresolved;
It's a code that must be solved.
Is her mind a small computer
Tuned to find the perfect suitor?

Does it measure dots and dashes,
Intervals between the flashes?
Could her head just know instinctively
What is being said so blinktively?

Scientists are still not sure
How she reads his signature.
Still she knows who telegraphed her,
And they'll live happily ever after. ◆

Axolotl

If you should catch an axolotl
Stick him quickly in a bottle.
He's not poison, he won't bite
But he might put up a squirmy fight.
He's just a kind of salamander;
A million things are finer, grander.
He'll slither, slide and wildly scuttle:
No place to hide, no place to huddle.
He'll try to climb the glass and fail
And fall back hard upon his tail.
He'll scamper, scared,'round and about,
Quivering, fidgeting, wanting OUT!
So, may I suggest, if you care a tottle
You turn him loose. Bye, axolotl! ◆

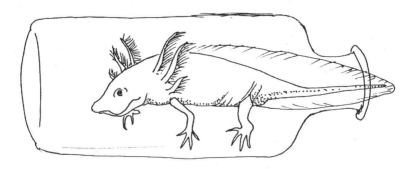

PART TWO
Critters of the Sea and Shore

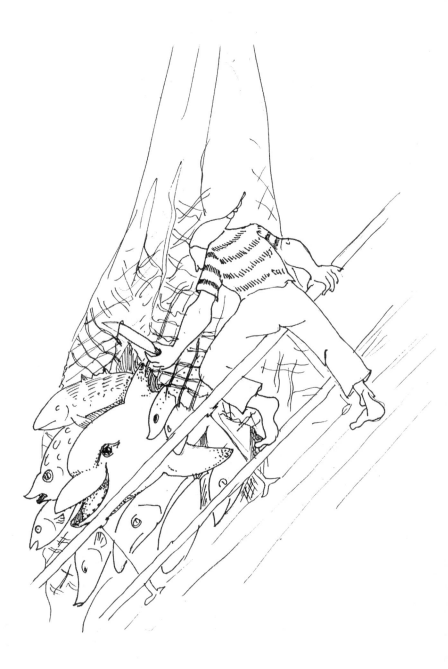

The Sailor's Tale

Chapter One

One night a young sailor was standing alone
On the deck of a fishing boat, dreaming of home
When a wild wave spawned by an undertide
Crested and tumbled him over the side.

The rest of the crew were at poker below
As the ship sailed blindly toward Mexico.
He shouted for help but a clap of thunder
Smothered the sound. Then his head went under.

Like many a sailor he couldn't swim
So Davy Jones' Locker was waiting for him.
He was floundering, drowning, his mind fading out
When his body was nudged by what felt like a snout.

There followed a bump, then a gentle nuzzle.
Whatever it was had a smooth, slick muzzle.
Then, Whack! He was lifted up out of the black
And found himself smack on a dolphin's back.

It let out a high-pitched, chittering squeak.
Did it mean "Hold Tight" in dolphin speak?
All right! He was grateful enough for the ride.
Then he noticed a little one close by her side.

And clearing his lungs, he wondered if maybe
She'd forced him to breathe like a new born baby.
For dolphins are mammals, a mammal needs air—
Be it mouse or moose or millionaire.

"She's a mermaid, a Nereid, she's Neptune's kin,"
He fancied. Both hands gripped her dorsal fin
As she playfully breached with an effortless motion
And sailed through the air, then ducked back to the ocean.

The little one, bred of courage and nerve,
Followed them perfectly, leap for curve.
No human invention could ever outdo
The way they swam and the way they flew.

Tenderly, kindly, his weight she bore
'Til she carried him close to the Mexican shore.
Then she tossed him away and he found he could stand
And wade to safety on clean, white sand.

He told his story that night in a bar
But they hooted and called him a "rumcrazy tar".
Then back with the fishermen, fearing their jeers,
He said he'd been saved by some drug racketeers.

Chapter Two

The years went by and the memory dimmed,
As rich were the waters their big nets skimmed.
Then came a time when for some strange reason
Their catch fell off at the height of the season.

The men were growly, the men were grumbly;
Their wives and their children at home were hungry.
"I'll find you some fish," the big mate swore
And, coming about, they headed offshore.

"Well, where are the fish?" the men were pleading
When splashes to port told of heavy ones feeding.
The sails were lowered, a sea anchor set,
As they tossed out their largest and strongest net.

When the winches groaned it was plain to them all
They were boating a bountiful, near record haul.
There was albacore, tuna and amberjack.
The mate said, "I'm buying a Cadillac."

But the sailor who once had been saved from drowning
Found himself watching carefully, frowning,
For something was wrong. In the midst of the splashing,
Terrified fish, a dolphin was thrashing.

He saw her struggle, he saw
	her heave,
She was slowly strangling, she could
	not breathe.
Then her eyes met his and they seemed
	to say,
"You owe me one, friend, and it's time to pay."

He pulled out his knife and without thinking twice
Rushed to the net and sliced a deep slice.
The loops unraveled, they split, they tore.
Some tuna escaped, then more and more,

'Til the net that a moment before had been filled,
Like a popped balloon, collapsed and spilled.
The dolphin broke free and she dived for the deep
To a place for forgetting, for healing, for sleep.

"Fare thee well," said the sailor. "We're even, my friend."
What a wonderful way for a tale to end.
But, no! Any act has a consequence
And this one would lead into violence.

Chapter Three

When the net came aboard with a final heft
A few small herring were all that were left.
A terrible fury came over the crew
And their angry looks turned on you-know-who.

"I'm sorry," he said. "You must surely forgive—
But I had to make sure that the dolphin would live.
I thought, well, I thought I could recognize
A mother's kindness in her eyes."

The mate stood above him, his hands on his hips.
His face was all red and tight were his lips.
He shouted, "You fool! Do you think that was funny?
You've lost every man here a passel of money.

"Don't pout like a puppy, all soupy-eyed.
You're going to pay for it out of your hide.
I'm breaking one bone for each fish in that catch."
Now the mate was more than the sailor's match.

A powerful right landed hard on the chin.
A left to the cheek tore open the skin.
He punched and he pummeled ferociously, madly,
'Til the sailor was down and bleeding badly.

It was plain he was done; his spirits were low
As the mate rushed in for the final blow,
Smirking a nasty, conqueror's smirk,
When all of a sudden the ship took a jerk.

As though some gargantuan fingers had gripped it
And shook it and tossed it and playfully tipped it.
The mate was off balance; he stumbled and tripped
And over the rail like a tiddlywink flipped.

(Now what was the cause of the ship's sudden pitch?
Well, a whale was under there scratching an itch.
For barnacles tickle and whales often steal
A scrape down the back from a ship's iron keel.)

"We've a man overboard," the Captain cried.
"All hands! Launch the dinghy over the side."
For the mate was another who couldn't swim;
If they didn't come quickly his chances were slim.

Then it seemed that the blighter was all out of luck:
The davits were rusty, the dory got stuck:
A very unfortunate roll of the dice
He was under three times, he was up only twice.

When the dinghy was freed and hit down with a plunk
Not a bubble broke where the mate had sunk.
Some sailors were cursing, some bowing to pray
Then they bent to their oars and rowed sadly away.

But what was that shape heading fast, coming in?
An ominous outline, a tall gray fin.
"A shark!" someone cried. "He's come for the mate—
Living or dead, it's a horrible fate."

The fin disappeared and they sucked in their breath
For all men will flinch in the presence of death.
They shivered and watched for the bright blood to spread
And color the water. Instead . . . instead . . .

A dolphin rose and across her back
The mate was sprawled like a gunny sack.
They lifted him in but his limbs were like jelly;
His skin was as pale as a pompano's belly.

Not a man said a word as they started to row.
They might have been thinking that no one can know
What fate will await at the morning tide.
Then they noticed the dolphin was still alongside.

She was circling the skiff like a dutiful mother.
They thought: Any dolphin looks quite like another.
It couldn't be true that the one who was freed
Is haunting us now as a taunt to our greed.

Then she stretched out her neck and peeked over the side
As if to make sure that the mate had died
And though, 'til that moment, there'd been little doubt
He lifted a hand and he patted her snout.

Then, flip! she was off in a high, leaping arc
As if it had all been a glorious lark.
She never was seen in those waters again
But her memory's sacred to sailor men. ◆

The Hermit Crab

A hermit crab was feeling unwell
Then he realized he had outgrown his shell.
When he'd first crawled inside, it had fit him just right
But now that he'd grown, it was plainly too tight.
There was nothing to do but to venture outside
And find a more spacious one where he could hide.

He squirmed his anatomy into the clear
And, suddenly naked, he shivered in fear.
For this was his nightmare: his dreams were obsessed
By the terror of crawling around all undressed.
A seagull was spiraling overhead;
If it spotted him now he was plain good as dead.

He crawled to the tide line and what met his eyes
But a conical shell that was perfect in size.
It was sanded pure white, so it wasn't alive
And he made a run for it, took a dive
And bumped his forehead and scratched his chin
On the claw of something most probably kin,

Which spoke, as he tumbled back bruised and shaken,
"Forget it, old chap, this one's already taken."
Then scuttling, scrabbling, combing the beach
He felt the gull's shadow, heard the gull's screech.
Translation: "Hooray! Here's a catch I can snatch
Unless it heads straight for the bulrushes patch."

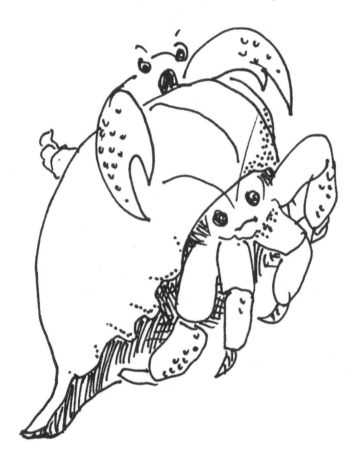

Can crustaceans "head straight"? Well, for once this one did
'Til the gull couldn't see what the tall grasses hid.
And safe for the moment the hermit crab rested,
So weary, so wan, but, so far, undigested.
But what was that sniffing and what was that crunch?
A hungry raccoon was out looking for lunch.

A black and white mask rose up over a rise.
As the gull had relied on his marvelous eyes
The coon was in tune with his sensitive nose
And a crab has a smell that is not like a rose.
The coon said, "Kasniggle, kasnoggle, kasneel."
Translation: "I think I have found me a meal."

The hermit crab perfectly understood
He scooted and skittered as fast as he could
'Til he spotted a shell at the back of a dune
As round and as pale as a full winter moon.
No time left for dawdling, for trying it on;
A squiggle, a plip and the crab was gone.

It was fine. It was roomy. A treasure; a plum;
And his claw made a perfect operculum
As the one who had fashioned the shell to begin with
Had a natural foot that he'd tuck himself in with.
The crab snuggled down and he plugged up the door
And had you been near you'd have heard a soft snore. ◆

The Shark and the Grouper

A young Mako shark was out on the hunt
Chasing a fat little blue striped grunt
When boaters above on a beerdrinking ride
Dumped all their garbage down over the side.

Along with the trash were those round plastic rings
That bind up a sixpack: they're dangerous things,
At least to this shark, for one circled his snout
Like a big rubber band and he couldn't get out.

He thrashed and he snuffled, this fish was a fighter
But all of his struggles just made it fit tighter.
He couldn't chew and he couldn't swallow;
His stomach was getting awfully hollow.

He'd sunk to the bottom, a terminal case,
When a grouper swam up with a smile on his face.
(Now, don't blame the grouper, his mouth is so wide
That he always looks sunny and undignified.)

He asked, "What's the matter?" The shark only whined
But the grouper could see he was caught in a bind.
And though he'd no fingers, no talons, no paws,
He was blessed with remarkably generous jaws.

So he chomped on the rings and he back-finned like mad.
He used every smidgen of strength that he had.
He tugged and he tussled to undo the noose
Then he back-somersaulted when, Pop! it turned loose.

"Well, now," said the grouper, "you owe me a smile."
The shark only grumbled, "A smile's not my style.
You're cute and you're kind, but I'm stronger, I'm braver.
So maybe some day I can pay back the favor.

While the shark grew tremendous and didn't stop growing,
The grouper stayed chubby and still easygoing.
They lived near a reef where once in a while
The shark would cruise by—grouper'd flash him a smile.

Though he'd never known hunger, he'd never known fear,
A danger was coming; its face would appear
As a human invading the sea from the land
With a tank on his back and a spear in his hand.

The grouper'd not seen such a creature before,
And, curious always, he went to explore.
He sidled up close, unaware of a threat,
Like a friendly Dalmatian expecting a pet.

The spearman thought, "Gracious, this fish is so tame
I'll soon have my dinner." He paused to take aim
But before he could strike, something swooshed through
    the sea
Coming fast as a Porsche at the Paris Grand Prix.

A shark! Now it swerved with such masterful grace
That it stopped smack in front of the speardiver's face.
It chose not to bite but its eerie eyes stared
And no human has lived who was ever so scared.

The message was plain: "Leave that grouper alone
Or you won't have a limb you can call your own."
The man dropped his spear, kicking wildly, hell bent
For his own, his less fearsome environment.

The shark let him go but, then purely for fun
He snatched the guy's flippers off, one by one.
Then he turned to the grouper. "You need some advice.
It's a real tough world; don't be so nice.

"You mustn't act chummy toward bipeds with spears:
My species has lasted for millions of years.
And there's nothing about us that's cuddly or flirty.
We've always survived 'cause we're mean, down and dirty."

"But it's not my fault," said the grateful grouper,
"That I look like a made up circus trouper.
I've tried but I can't seem to manage a frown.
Whatever I do, I still look like a clown."

"Even so," said the shark. "If you don't learn to hide,
You'll end up as filet, either baked, broiled or fried.
But wait just a bit. Am I being too hasty?
There's no doubt at all you're nutritious and tasty.

"I will eat you myself! I'll enjoy every morsel
From your fat, juicy lips to the tip of your dorsal.
Here I come! See my teeth! You are in for a shock
Unless you swim fast to that hole in the rock."

The grouper swam fast, hearing jaws click behind him
And dived in the hole where the shark couldn't find him.
"That monster,' he thought, "was horrendously serious.
But what a strange change! It was all so mysterious."

(What he couldn't have seen from his safe and snug place
Was the flick of a smile on the shark's ugly face.) ◆

Aunt Ida and the Two Barracudas

I'll tell you the story of Aunt Ida Hayes.
I don't know exactly what Aunt Ida weighs;
It's close to three hundred, I'll venture to guess,
But she's chock full of energy, nevertheless.

Well, Aunt Ida Hayes is a pretty good swimmer:
She floats a lot better than folks who are slimmer.
But floating got boring; she soon took up Scuba
Wearing weights that were heavy enough to sink Cuba.

A lover of travel, she practiced her sport
On reefs around many an island resort.
And thus it occurred that one day off Bermuda
Aunt Ida met up with a big barracuda.

She'd finished a breakfast of two dozen kippers;
She'd gathered her mask and her tank and her flippers;
She'd rented a boat and rowed out to a place
Where the fish looked like angels, the coral like lace.

Adjusting her gear and the belt that would weight her,
She tested the draw on her new regulator,
Then flipped over backward—an old diver's trick
And with all of that lead she went down pretty quick.

Well, the big barracuda was not far away
And nothing had happened to brighten his day.
He was lazily cruising his territory
When down came Aunt Ida in all of her glory.

88

Now nothing's more rude than a big barracuda
To some uninvited, non-native intruder.
This fish wasn't hungry, an hour before
He'd eaten some squid and an albacore,

"So," he thought: "I'll give chase "til it runs out of breath
Then I'll show it my teeth and I'll scare it to death."
Then off on his terrorist tantrum he zoomed,
But the closer he got, the larger she loomed.

He couldn't believe the sight that he saw:
She looked like a float from the Mardi Gras;
She looked like a Clydesdale, a hippo, a moose;
She looked like a train, or at least a caboose;

She looked like a middle-sized submarine.
But none of these sights had he ever seen.
His vision, it happens, was not all that great
So he slowly edged close to investigate.

Now Aunt Ida didn't know what she should do.
With her mouthpiece in place, she could hardly say, "Boo!"
She shivered in fear from her head to her toes,
But all she could think of was thumbing her nose.

Now the fish was approaching from underneath
And her wiggling fingers looked somehow like teeth.
Oh, he had no fear of a manta ray;
He'd tackle a swordfish any old day;

He'd nibbled the tail of a whale for a lark;
He'd eaten an octopus. Oh, but a shark!
A shark was "The Boss" and he held that position
By dint of his truly amazing dentition.

Could this be a shark of some yet un-met species?
If so, better go—he could end up in pieces.
He swiftly departed. Aunt Ida returned
To her beach front hotel, not real sure what she'd learned.

She'd ask other divers to help with explaining
And thought, "For tonight, I'll be quite entertaining."
So, she dined upon lobster and veal cacciatore
And paused between courses to narrate her story.

Dessert was a caramel almond soufflé,
And she took her sweet time going over her day.
But at last, choosing fruit and a half pound of Gouda,
She told how she'd frightened a big barracuda.

A spiffy young lady who was plumb undersized,
Said, "Dahling, I'm not in the least bit surprised.
In fact, I can almost feel sorry for him:
He'd never before seen an elephant swim."

The tourists giggled and snickered and muttered
And those with their mouths full, dribbled or sputtered.
Fat folk are so often the butt of a joke,
She couldn't be blamed if she'd wished they'd all choke.

But though she was hurting, she'd not let it show;
So she turned to the lady. "There's one thing I know.
There are creatures on shore who have manners
        more vicious
Than those in the sea. My! This cheese is delicious." ◆

A True Story — January 1990

This happened in Arkansas one bitter day
When some good old boys went out to play
And shoot them some ducks. But the water was frozen
And the lake where they squatted no duckies had chosen.

They sort of got bored, so they thought if they'd clear
A nice open pond then some birds might appear
And set theirselves down for a rest and a drink
So one of the group said, "Now, lookie, I think

"That a small stick of dynamite might do the job."
They agreed and they lit one. A masterful lob
Set it sailing a goodly ways over the ice
And, merrily fizzling, it landed real nice.

They'd just plain forgotten their golden retriever,
Well-bred and well-trained and a super achiever.
She bounced up delighted and headed hell bent
Out over the lake to return what they'd sent.

With the joy of the chase, true and blue to her kind
She picked up the stick and turned back toward the blind.
The men thought of running but manlike they stayed.
"If she jes' keeps acomin'," said one, "shoot her daid."

But why should she stop? She was playing their game
And, silky ears flopping, gallumping she came.
Aquiver with pleasure, now faster and faster
Determined to offer her prize to her master.

Yes, the love of good dogs is the code of the South
But the sparkles were twinkling alongside her mouth.
So her owner, now panicked was losing his cool,
"All together," he sputtered, "let's kill the dern fool."

They lifted their guns for the dire deed to do
But before they could fire them, the dynamite blew.
The dog was a goner, alas and alack!
Still I can't help but wish she had first made it back.

. The End

Ann Heiskell Rickey was born in Memphis, Tennessee in 1919, where she lives with her husband of fifty years, Albert Clifton Rickey. She attended Saint Mary's School For Girls, Randolph Macon Womens' College, and the University of Tennessee. She has been active in politics and was an elected member of the Tennessee Democratic Party Executive Committee for 20 years, as well as a delegate to two National Democratic Party Conventions. Her hobby has always been travel, and lured by her fascination with peoples and places, she has circled the globe from Botswana to Borneo. For several years she sailed the Caribbean on a 53-foot Alden schooner.